Tiny World

Terrariums

Tiny  World
Terrariums

A STEP-BY-STEP GUIDE TO EASILY CONTAINED LIFE

FROM THE CREATORS OF TWIG TERRARIUMS

MICHELLE INCIARRANO
& KATY MASLOW

PHOTOGRAPHS BY ROBERT WRIGHT

STC CRAFT / A MELANIE FALICK BOOK / STEWART, TABORI & CHANG
NEW YORK

Contents

Introduction:
The Story of Twig
Terrariums
PAGE 6

A Brief History of
Terrariums
PAGE 10

What Kind of Terrarium
Will You Make?
PAGE 14

Let's Get Terrarin'
PAGE 24

Terrariums Galore
PAGE 50

Resources
PAGE 116

About the Authors
PAGE 118

Acknowledgments
PAGE 119

Introduction

{ The Story of Twig Terrariums }

"The soil is the great connector of our lives,
the source and destination of all."

—Wendell Berry, *The Unsettling of America*, 1977

Twig Terrariums, our Brooklyn-based terrarium company, all started with a glass container and the crafty passion of two old friends. For years, we had been getting crafty together once a week, making bookmarks and greeting cards. But one day Michelle bought a small glass cruet and randomly decided that its destiny was to become a terrarium. It was very important to her that she had all the info necessary to make a healthy terrarium inside the tiny jar she adored. She started her quest for directions online and brought her findings to her college chemistry professor to make sure she hadn't missed anything. Happy, sprightly moss soon made itself at home within the cruet.

Katy soon followed suit, inspired by Michelle's enthusiasm and a little vintage mushroom jar she found at an antiques store in Englishtown, New Jersey. We loved how the terrariums looked so much like wonderful little gardens, and that's when we had the idea to populate them with miniatures and figurines. The small mushroom jar was soon inhabited by a band of hobos roasting weenies 'round a campfire. And Michelle's cruet came to house a couple of young adventurers exploring their terrain.

One terrarium begat others, and soon we had completely abandoned making bookmarks and greeting cards on craft nights. The hunt for cool figurines was in full swing, and we experimented with different moisture levels, soils, and moss to be sure we got it just right. Our small Brooklyn apartments became jam-packed with dozens of terrariums and glass containers of all shapes and sizes. Soon it became clear that we needed to start moving those terrariums out of our apartments, so we decided to try our hand at selling them. But first, we needed a name for our company. Weeks of brainstorming ensued (some contenders included Peepshow Terrariums and Grow Terrariums—boring!), and oodles of logo ideas were passed back and forth.

Frustrated, but still having fun, we hit Prospect Park in beautiful Brooklyn to relax in the sunshine and take a break from thinking. When lo! What should lie within reach of our lounging bodies but a lone twig . . . a perfect, knotty, excellent twig. And we just knew it: Twig Terrariums was born! (We still have the twig that inspired it all.)

Our first decision as Twig Terrariums' proprietors was to set up a booth at the illustrious Brooklyn Flea, a local market that Katy had heard was the bee's knees for aspiring artists and crafters. Our first time selling at the Flea was a lovely April day, and the crowds just ate us up! We never expected such a huge response, nor that a writer from the *New York Times* would happen along and spot our wares. The rest is history—from there on out, we knew that our moss nerdiness had a destiny.

The future of Twig quickly took shape. Soon after the *Times* article hit with its big, bright pictures of our miniature worlds, e-mails and orders came flooding in. We moved our mossy operation from our respective dining-room tables to a cute studio in a converted garage on a quiet block near Prospect Park. We began creating commissioned pieces, introduced DIY kits that we shipped all around the country, and started offering workshops and events around town. Local stores reached out to us, asking to carry our unique creations, and after one year, we even had to move into a bigger studio.

But this book is not about us—it's about *you*, and how you can start making terrariums, too! For city folk like us with nary a fire escape, terrariums are a way to bring a "plot of land" into the home. But no matter where you live, terrariums are therapeutic to create and peaceful to observe. Everything you need to know about making your very own tiny world is right here. From picking plants and containers to assembling your terrariums, we walk you through each step of the way. Plus, we show you how to make each one extra special by creating quirky worlds with figurines and miniatures to mimic people's real lives and interests. With *Tiny World Terrariums*, we hope to share our love of little green worlds with everyone. Read on, verdant friends.

Michelle Inciarrano

Katy Maslow

{ A Brief History of }
Terrariums

pteridomania {noun} "fern fever": a term
coined in 1855 by Charles Kingsley in reference
to the Victorian fern-collecting craze

A terrarium, by definition, is a transparent enclosure for keeping or growing plants. The container allows plants to remain in their original soil, maintain their own air climate, and stay moist. There are two types of terrariums: closed terrariums, which allow plants and mosses with higher moisture needs to thrive, and open terrariums for those plants that require a drier environment. The first terrarium on record was accidentally discovered in England in 1829 by Nathaniel Ward, and this discovery revolutionized how plants could be maintained in low-humidity conditions. Ward's garden in Wellclose Square housed many different types of ferns—a passion inspired by a trip to Jamaica—but the plants were dying from the coal smoke and sulfuric acid that were polluting the air of nineteenth-century London. At the time,

Ward was also collecting moth cocoons in small bottles, and he noticed a few fern spores were thriving in small bits of soil in the bottles. He had a carpenter build a small glass case (which became known as a "Wardian case") and filled it with soil and ferns to test his hypothesis. Surprise! The ferns flourished in the glass container with little to no care provided by Ward himself.

Ward's discovery was the product of a series of chance events, for sure. Without these chance events, who knows how long the world would have had to wait to enjoy terrariums?

The Victorian era was chock-full of botanical discoveries. The ability to transport plants across land and sea made it possible to study them outside of their native lands, and Ward's discovery prompted a 90 percent increase in plant transport. Thousands of new hybrid plants were introduced and many advances in biological studies were made: from the work of Charles Darwin, who was an avid botanist, to that of Gregor Mendel, who published a study that pioneered plant genetics, to Ward himself, who had visions of using botany to help the sick, elderly, and mentally ill (today, this is called horticultural therapy, and it's used worldwide as an effective rehabilitation tool). Needless to say, the number of botanical studies taking place in this era was incredible, eventually leading to monumentally important things like the discovery of penicillin and the advent of the world-wide tea industry! (The Wardian case made possible the first successful transport of twenty thousand tea seedlings from China in 1843.) As the Wardian case evolved and gained popularity, its name changed to "terrarium," derived from the Latin *terra*, meaning land, and *arium*, abstracted from "aquarium."

Now fast-forward to the fun and funky 1970s, when things were . . . not so fresh! Environmental issues came to the forefront in the early seventies in response to a growing concern over the health and well-being of our delicate and mistreated ecosystem. With the creation of the Environmental Protection Agency, the start of Greenpeace, and the signing of the Endangered Species Act, the environment became a topic of conversation in every home and classroom. With ecosystems on everyone's minds, terrariums became a huge hit because they were a way of bringing the outside in! Dozens of books came out on the subjects of container gardening and terrarium making. Many modern terrarium enthusi-asts come to us with nostalgic tales of making terrar-iums in their elementary school classrooms or at their kitchen tables with their moms.

Today, terrariums are making a huge comeback. In fact, these aesthetically pleasing ecosystems are cropping up as lead players in the décor of homes,

restaurants, stores, and offices, pushing indoor gardening to a new level. High-end interior designers have started using terrariums as substi-tutes for houseplants, and terrariums have become a design must-have for nature lovers who want some low-maintenence greenery in their homes. After all, terrariums are not just another collection of houseplants; they are easily contained, easily maintained . . . life.

ABOVE: A Wardian case housing English ivy.

{ What Kind of }
Terrarium
Will You Make?

terrarable {adj}: **perfect for housing a terrarium;**
"This vase is totally terrarable."

HERMAN THE CAT shares his windowsill perch with this open, succulent terrarium, which thrives in a sunny spot.

BEFORE YOU GET STARTED ON ANY TERRARIUM-MAKING ADVENTURE, you have to ask yourself a few questions: Where will the terrarium go? What kind of plant or container do you want to use? Your answers will help determine what kind of terrarium you should make. Note that the soil, container, and lighting requirements depend on the type of plant you choose, so make these decisions before you buy your ingredients.

WHERE WILL THE TERRARIUM GO?

If you are making a terrarium intended for a specific location—such as a sunny windowsill or a dark basement apartment—the environmental conditions of that location will determine the type of plant and container you choose. If your terrarium is destined for a sunny spot, you'll need to use a sun-loving houseplant or a succulent and use a container with a wide opening. If the setting will be shady (or mostly shady), you will be better off making a moss or fern terrarium with a closed container (or one with a very narrow opening) since they thrive in low-light conditions.

WHAT KIND OF PLANT DO YOU WANT TO USE?

Terrariums can house a variety of plants, but maybe you prefer the look of moss over succulents? Or perhaps you fancy more traditional houseplants? No matter what type of plant you choose, make sure that you are putting it in the right type of container and that it will live in an environment that will make it happy (see the chart below for an overview). If you have kitties (or kids, for that matter) who love eating plants, it's also important to choose plants that aren't poisonous and won't cause skin irritation. We recommend doing a quick Internet search before introducing any type of plant into a home.

WHAT KIND OF CONTAINER DO YOU WANT TO USE?

If you have a particular container in mind that you want to use for your terrarium, this will dictate what type of plant you use. If it has a lid or a narrow opening, you will need to make a moss terrarium. If your container has a wide opening, you would be better off making a succulent or plant terrarium.

	MOSS	SUCCULENT	OTHER PLANTS (SEE PAGE 40)
CONTAINER	Closed	Open, short walls	Open, tall walls
SOIL	Peat moss mixture	Sandy	Potting mix
LIGHT	Shade	Sun	Depends on plant
CARE	Mist approximately every 2 to 4 weeks	Water every other week (and more in hot temperatures)	Depends on plant

EVEN THE TINIEST OF glass containers need headspace so your plants can breathe.

CONTAINERS: THREE GOLDEN RULES

Containers for terrariums should optimally be made from glass because it is clear and tends to maintain a consistent temperature. When picking suitable glass for a terrarium, there are three major things to consider: transparency, airflow, and headroom, so the plants can breathe.

TRANSPARENCY: The glass you choose for a terrarium must be clear. It may be slightly tinted, such as recycled glass (which usually has a blue or green cast), but fully colored glass will not allow the right light spectrum to penetrate the container, which plants need in order to be happy. This is especially true of green glass, in which plants will not grow (according to Michelle's chemistry professor at Brooklyn College).

AIRFLOW: The amount of airflow needed will depend on how moist the plant likes to be, and airflow is determined by the size of the terrarium's opening. For most moss terrariums, the container must have a lid or a small opening so that moisture stays inside; that way, the terrarium can monitor its own moisture, and you will only have to check on it every few weeks. In contrast, shade-loving plants (like peacock spikemoss and asparagus ferns) need containers with larger openings since they don't like to be as moist as moss.

HEADROOM: Sure, great terrarable glass can be as small as a salt shaker or a vintage Chanel Nº 5 bottle (as shown at left). But whatever you fancy, you'll need to reserve some headspace at the top—usually about half of the container—to retain enough air to keep moss or plants healthy. Containers for succulents should have no walls at all, or very low ones at most so the glass doesn't fry the succulents or retain so much moisture that they rot.

A NOTE ON PLASTIC: Plastic terrariums aren't totally out of the question—there are some super fun and funky containers from the 1970s that we love. But we've found that plastic reacts differently in changing temperatures and usually produces a lot more condensation than glass, which makes them trickier to maintain.

TYPES OF GLASS

Glass is the optimal material for terrarium containers, and there are lots of types available. We like to use repurposed glass when possible, but almost any transparent glass will do the job.

---

1 ANTIQUE AND VINTAGE GLASS: We love to use existing materials in order to reduce the use of new raw materials, and terrariums can be a perfect way to upcycle glass. According to antiques experts (the upcycling gurus), glass must be more than one hundred years old to be considered "antique." Glass more than twenty but less than one hundred years old is "vintage." Antique and vintage containers tend to have minor defects, such as air bubbles from old manufacturing processes, or nicks from having been around the block, but this can lend to their charm. A vintage pickle jar, an antique apothecary jar, an old compote bowl with lid (or without, if you're using succulents), or even an old Mason jar . . . all of these are great terrarable finds.

2 RECYCLED GLASS: Most recycled glass comes from two places: Spain and Italy. Spanish recycled glass has a very pretty aqua tint to it, while Italian recycled glass tends to have a greenish cast. Don't worry, the tint is subtle enough to let light filter through. Both types are beautiful and look great as a terrarium! Some vessels have cork lids, which can add to their charm (and practicality). There are varying degrees of quality in recycled glass, and it's usually best to look at the item in person before purchasing. Some of this glass is thick and hard to see through— thin, transparent recycled glass is preferable. It can be

very hard to tell the difference online, and photos can sometimes misrepresent the real thing.

3 NEW GLASS: If you find a new piece of glass in your favorite store that would be perfect for your terrarium, then you may not want to look further. That's okay! With all the new glass products out there, it's easy to find something you like without breaking the piggy bank or searching high and low in antiques shops.

4 CRYSTAL: If you don't mind the high price tag, crystal is an elegant way to house a terrarium. Crystal vessels are usually perfectly clear. Lead is added to glass in order to create many types of crystal containers, and this is what gives it significantly more shine and makes it so clear. However, this also makes the glass softer, and we've been told that the higher the lead content, the more likely it is to shatter. For this reason, we recommend that crystal terrariums be kept away from children, but we bet you knew that already.

5 HANDBLOWN GLASS: Handblown glass terrarium containers are available in more unique shapes than traditionally manufactured glass containers. It is also possible to ask a glassblower to customize a terrarium just for you. It's an expensive option, but the results can be amazing.

1 VINTAGE COTTON BALL JAR

2 VINTAGE DECANTER

3 RECYCLED GLASS VASE

4 VINTAGE HEISLEY CREAMER

5 NEW GLASS
   BIRD-TOPPED
   APOTHECARY JAR

6 NEW GLASS
   APOTHECARY JAR

THIS LOW-WALLED compote dish serves as the perfect base for three camels in a desert oasis.

THE FACTORS YOU NEED TO CONSIDER WHEN CHOOSING A CONTAINER VARY DEPENDING ON THEY TYPE OF PLANT YOU'RE USING IN YOUR TERRARIUM. Generally speaking, however, it helps to choose glass with a tall, cylindrical shape. When you're evaluating container size, keep in mind that you'll want the terrarium to be half full or less when it's complete so that air can circulate in the top half; for this reason, shallow containers tend not to work as well. You'll also find it best to stay away from decanters, however tempting they may be, as their bulbous shape and narrow neck tend to retain too much moisture.

Here are some other rules of thumb to keep in mind that pertain to specific plant types:

MOSS AND MOISTURE-LOVING SHADE PLANTS: Use a container with a lid, or one with a small opening in any shape or size. While we delight in hard-to-make terrariums with openings barely a half inch (12 millimeters) wide, not everyone feels up to this challenge, and a container with an opening smaller than three inches (7.5 centimeters) shouldn't be attempted until you've had some practice. When first starting out, look for wide-mouth containers—ones you can fit your hand into—and top it off with a lid.

SUCCULENTS: Although succulents are hardwired to live for extended periods of time in less-than-ideal conditions, moisture will eventually rot the little fellas, killing them over a span of several months. There's also the matter of light: Succulents LOVE sunlight, but receiving light through glass magnifies the rays and effectively creates a little solar oven that will cook your poor succulents, so containers with low walls (or no walls) work best. There are several great pedestal glass pieces that will make a really healthy home for these plants, or you could go for a nifty clear compote dish.

SUN-LOVING PLANTS: For any plant terrarium that is going to get lots of sun, don't choose a container that will encase the plants. Most plants can be terrared in a variety of open containers, and finding them is a breeze! Think large brandy glasses or lidless cookie jars or sturdy vintage crystal bowls.

{ Let's Get }
Terrarin'

terrar {verb}: to create a terrarium;
"We terrared all day."

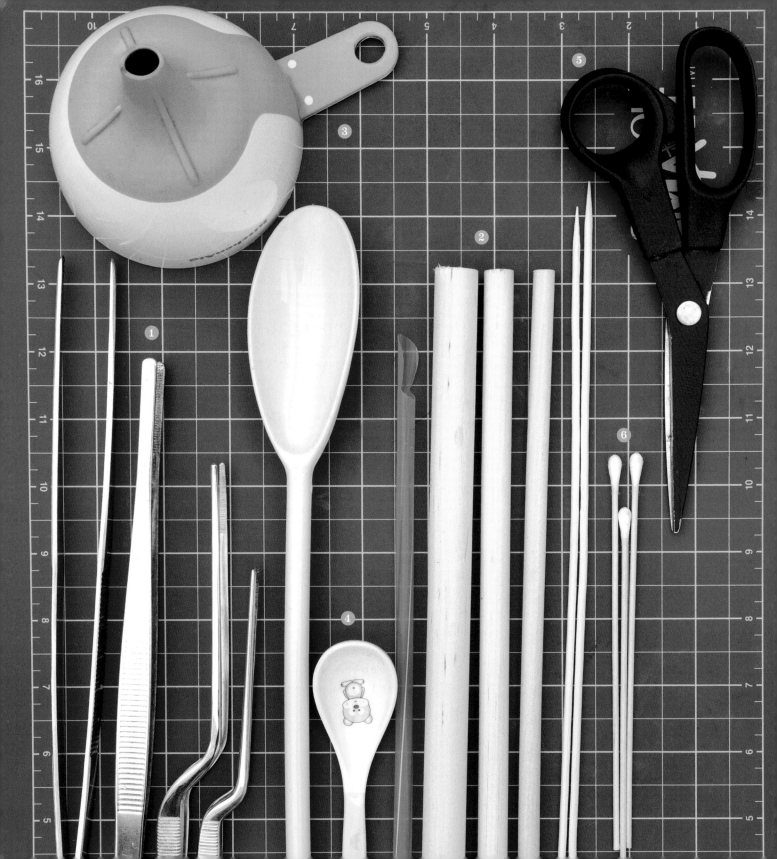

BASIC TOOLS

Before you start building your terrarium, there are a few tools you'll need to gather. Here is a list of the tools we always keep on our worktable at Twig. Almost all of these tools can be found in hardware or discount stores, or check the Resources on page 116.

1 TWEEZERS OF ALL SHAPES AND SIZES: Tweezers are great for placing materials (moss, rocks, or even a figurine) in an exact location. We use a variety of long, short, straight, and angled tweezers to work with different-size containers. Look for foot-long tweezers; they will be your best friend for terrarin' all those hard-to-reach spots!

2 POKEY STICKS: Available in many forms, pokey sticks are among the most useful terrarin' tools. Thin dowels work best for arranging moss, while wide dowels are best for tamping down your filtration and soil layers. Skewers or chopsticks can be used in place of dowels, especially when you're working with a super-tiny container. For the really crazy container shapes, we sometimes use computer technician and car mechanic tools, such as bendy "mechanical fingers" that can really get into the corners of a glass vessel.

3 FUNNELS: Funnels will keep you from making a mess when adding soil or rocks to a small-necked container. Have a bunch on hand in various sizes.

4 SPOONS: Spoons of all sizes come in handy when you're mini-scaping (see page 42). We've even been known to hold spoons with clamps to form an über-long spoon, which can help get rocks snug up against the glass. When making a succulent terrarium, it's helpful to use a long spoon to deposit sand or dirt. Then use a straw to blow any excess dirt or debris from the plants.

5 SCISSORS: These are handy for shearing off clumps of moss.

6 PAPER TOWELS AND SWABS: Cleaning the glass inside the terrarium can be difficult sometimes, especially if the terrarium's opening is tiny. You can use a long, wet swab or fashion one using a chopstick or tweezers and a wet paper towel to get in those hard-to-reach places.

LAYER 1: ROCKS

Whether you are using moss, succulents, or plants,
every terrarium begins with a layer of rocks.

THE LANDSCAPE OF YOUR TINY WORLD BEGINS WITH A LAYER OF ROCKS, which shapes the terrain and allows for drainage and aeration. If you want a small hill or valley in your finished terrarium, arrange your rocks accordingly.

Many decorative rocks, such as polished pebbles, marble chips, pea gravel, blue gems, and beach glass, work well as a base and can even be layered to create some neat special effects. If you are collecting rocks from the great outdoors, be sure to wash them well and let them dry. This will help keep diseases or pests at bay in your new terrarium. Any rocks that can fit through the opening of your terrarium will work. We often use small polished pebbles, which are great for drainage and don't put too much pressure on the glass, but feel free to use marbles or manufactured rocks

instead. Just stay away from sand; it doesn't properly aerate the container.

While moss terrariums are not watered the same way as plant or succulent terrariums, they all need drainage and aeration. The amount of rocks you need will vary depending on the size of the vessel. As shown in the photo above, some tiny glass containers will require a thin layer of pea gravel, while the rock layer in large jars and containers can be several inches thick. Just remember that when all the layers are added, your terrarium needs room to breathe, so don't get too rock-crazed.

When working with this layer, always set aside a few rocks to use later when you're mini-scaping your terrarium.

LAYER 2: FILTRATION

THE FILTRATION LAYER FORMS A BARRIER THAT KEEPS YOUR SOIL FROM FALLING INTO THE DRAINAGE LAYER, which helps keep the terrarium from gettin' funky! We recommend a low-quality dried moss, which you can typically find at hardware and garden-supply stores. Usually labeled sphagnum or sheet moss, it comes in large bags.

To use dried moss, take a handful and soak it in water for a few seconds, then wring it out thoroughly; slightly damp is okay, but you don't want to introduce any more moisture than that into the terrarium. After wringing out the moss, flatten it into a pancake and push it down over the rock layer. This filtration layer must cover the rocks completely in order to keep your next layer, the soil, from seeping into your drainage area. Use a pokey stick to push the moss into any crevices and tamp it down. (If the terrarium's opening is large enough, you can also use a thick dowel or the handle of a trowel to tamp down the moss.)

CHARCOAL: Some people like to use charcoal to filter the air and water in a terrarium, but we tend to enjoy the fresh smell of earth inside each terrarium (as long as it's not funky!), which charcoal removes. Feel free to use charcoal or leave it out as you prefer. If you add charcoal, a thin layer, sprinkled between the rocks and the filtration moss layer, is perfect.

LAYER 3: SOIL

Terrariums are moist environments by nature, and soil plays a big role in keeping things that way. Introducing the wrong kind of soil can wreak havoc on this little ecosystem, so heed the advice below, and your terrarium will be the happier for it. When you add soil, use a funnel for more controlled placement. Also keep in mind that this is the perfect time to continue shaping a hill, slope, or valley by arranging the soil accordingly.

MOSS TERRARIUMS: We like to use a peat moss mixture for moss terrariums because of its low organic content, which makes the mix less likely to attract pests or form mold. The mixture is also able to retain a proper balance of moisture. Since moss does not have a root system, it anchors to the soil using threadlike growths called rhizoids. Your goal as terrarium maker is to make sure you have a good, thin layer of soil to cover the filtration layer, and to push down firmly on the moss to remove any air pockets between the soil and the rhizoids. You want to create a happy bond between the layers.

OTHER PLANT TERRARIUMS: The type of soil depends on the type of plants you use, but generally a good non-moisture-control potting mix will work fine. If you have plants that require a particular type of soil—such as an African violet mix or orchid bark for orchids—

it's best to buy a mix that works specifically for those plants. Whatever you do, do *not* buy moisture-control soil—it's unnecessary and will wind up creating a nasty, swampy mess in your terrarium. Be sure you use enough soil to cover the plant's root system, plus an inch or so for room to grow.

SUCCULENT TERRARIUMS: These require a more porous potting medium. You can buy a succulent mix at a local nursery or a hardware superstore, or you can make your own with two parts potting soil, one part perlite (a form of volcanic glass that is known to retain moisture and prevent soil compaction), and one part very coarse sand. Of course, by the time you buy all these ingredients it might be easier (and less expensive) to just grab a bag of the mix. Be sure to cover the roots and leave a little room for them to grow.

1 **ORCHID BARK**   3 **SUCCULENT MIX**

2 **PEAT MOSS MIX**   4 **POTTING SOIL MIX**

LAYER 4: PLANTS

Now it's time to add your live plants and piece the puzzle together.

MOSS: If you purchased your moss, it should be ready to use. If you've collected your moss from the great outdoors (see page 38), you'll need to make sure it's bug-free. Either spray the moss thoroughly with pesticide (we prefer organic products like Organocide) or dip it in a pesticide solution, then leave it in a bag or plastic container for at least a few hours. All the creepy-crawlies should be dead, and your moss will be ready for its new home. If you're like Michelle and are really grossed out by bugs, leave the moss in the bag for a day.

Once the moss has been de-bugged, use scissors to shear off chunks and play around with the height, texture, and shape of the terrain in your container. When you're happy with the placement of the moss, use a pokey stick to gently push it down and move it around. Be sure to press the moss down firmly to avoid air pockets between the moss and soil. That's it!

PLANTS AND SUCCULENTS: Plants and succulents need breathing room. You've probably seen terrariums for sale that have the plants close together, but these terrariums are in it for the short haul. Plants that are too close together can kill each other by strangling one another's roots or by blocking out the other's light. A little open pathway through a magical world is a very good thing.

When removing a plant from its original pot, be sure to gently knock off some of the soil attached to its roots and fluff them up a bit so they have an easier time adjusting to their new home. Place the plant in a shallow layer of soil and hold it upright while you scoop soil around it, then pat down the soil a little bit so the plant stays put and not too much air remains near the roots. Repeat with any other plants you're adding to your terrarium, then water (but do not drench) your new additions. A good, healthy watering will help prevent transplant shock, but you never want to add so much that the plant is sitting in a puddle. Remember: even though there are rocks on the bottom of the terrarium to prevent root rot, there are no actual drainage holes like those you'd find in a potted plant.

There is no doubt about it: We are total moss-o-philes!

FOR US TWIG CHICKS, IT ALL STARTED WITH THE MOSS TERRARIUM, so mosses have a special place in our twiggy hearts! We love moss in our terrariums for numerous reasons. Most important, we find it easy to care for! Moss thrives on neglect and poor light conditions, so it's perfect for our busy urban lifestyles, and because moss is slow growing, we don't have to worry too much about pruning. Moss also does not need to be fertilized since it requires little nutrition, and it can be very forgiving after a bout of dehydration. It's tough stuff. (The American Institute of Aeronautics and Astronautics actually suggested that moss might be used to terraform the moon into a sustainable living planet!) But perhaps best of all, moss makes a great landscape in which to create imaginary worlds. That makes it the bee's knees in our eyes.

Mosses belong to the division Bryophyta, which means that they are nonvascular plants and receive their nutrients through their leaves. Although mosses do not have true vascular tissue or a root system, they have rhizoids, threadlike filaments that anchor them to the ground. Many mosses grow closely crowded in mats or cushions on rocks or soil, while others grow on the trunks and leaves of forest trees.

Moss thrives in damp environments with low light; you can generally spy clumps in the wild along shady wooded areas and at the edges of streams. Once you actively seek out moss, you'll notice it everywhere! You can even find moss every now and then in the cracks of damp city streets or in culverts or drains.

There are more than fifteen thousand different types of moss, but looks can be deceiving. Some plants pose as moss because they're low lying and are soft and pretty. Beware: They may actually have a root system, which would not be good in a closed terrarium. Two examples of this type of poseur would be *Sagina subulata* (also known as Irish moss) and Spanish moss. And some moss only lives in water, such as Java moss or Christmas moss. Before including new moss in a terrarium, be sure to read about it. On the next four pages, you'll find information about some of our favorite mosses.

HAPPY MOSS

At Twig, we only use a few types of moss, all of which have similar soil conditions (so we know they will play well together). Out of the many mosses that have crossed our path, these are our favorites.

①

②

PILLOW or **CUSHION MOSS** (*Leucobryum glaucum*) is one of our favorites because of its brilliant green color and the way it grows in a tight clump so it resembles little hills. It can grow up to three inches (7.5 centimeters) tall and can form large mats several feet (about one meter) across.

SHEET MOSS or **HYPNUM MOSS** (*Hypnum cupressiforme*) is another favorite because it's easy to manipulate and can lie very low to the ground, growing only one half to four inches (12 millimeters to 10 centimeters) tall. This moss is seriously tough stuff! We hear it can be found on every continent, except Antarctica (understandable . . . brrr . . .).

We love using **SPHAGNUM MOSS** (*Sphagnum spp*) to make interesting tree shapes, but you generally won't find this moss in the woods. Sphagnum loves wet and boggy areas, and it's been said that several species of sphagnum can hold up to twenty times their weight in water! It can grow up to four inches (10 centimeters) tall in thick, dense clumps. You'll sometimes see this handsome fella on top of or under decaying material near ponds and streams. Note that sphagnum moss sold in bags at nurseries is usually dead and won't regrow—it's meant to be used as a filtration layer (see page 29), rather than a healthy, living top layer.

REINDEER MOSS (*Cladonia rangiferina*) can lend that otherworldly look to a terrarium. Although you'd think it's a moss from the English name, the Latin name gives it away (if you know anything about genus names): *Cladonia* means "cup lichen." This faux moss/lichen works great in moss terrariums. It's composed of a fungi and an algae that work symbiotically in one structure—the fungi benefits from the algae because fungi has no chlorophyll to synthesize its own food, while the algae benefits from the fungi's ability to absorb and retain water and nutrients. As the name suggests, reindeer love to munch on this delicate-looking beauty, and this hardy lichen is able to survive cold quite well. It has tendrils that branch out in several directions, making it look more like a pale green ethereal sponge than anything else.

THIS COUPLE DANCES THROUGH a jungle of mosses (pillow, mood, haircap, reindeer, and sphagnum), perfectly demonstrating how mosses can be combined to create a lush, varied world.

HAIRCAP MOSS (*Polytrichum juniperinum*) is found in sandier areas or next to burned logs. It is a great choice for creating a "tree" look. In fact, up close this moss looks just like a stand of tiny pine trees! We've seen some about two inches (5 centimeters) tall, but the height of this moss can vary depending on age, environment, and type. This variety is found on every continent and comes in shades of red as well as green.

And last, we should tackle the *Dicranum* genus, which refers to the windblown or fork mosses, like **MOOD MOSS** (shown above), **BROOM MOSS**, or **ROCK CAP MOSS**. It grows one to four inches (2.5 to 10 centimeters) tall and the stems rarely stand straight, which gives it that "blowin' in the wind" appearance. *Dicranum* tends to be a brighter green and definitely needs more shade than other mosses do to stay happy. And when it's happy it looks oh so happy!

ROAD TRIP!

Now that you know what to look for, let's go mossin'!

BE SURE TO GO MOSSING IN SAFE AREAS, SUCH AS ON YOUR OWN LAND OR A FRIEND'S. Don't be tempted to get your moss from parks and public spots—you could be fined or even arrested! Be careful not to take too much from one area when mossing—you want it to grow back. When you go mossing, don't forget:

1 A CELL PHONE AND COMPASS OR GPS: You don't want to wander too far off the beaten path. If you do, make sure you can get back to civilization or you may wind up as yeti food.

2 A TROWEL: Using this gardening tool, you'll be able to pull up moss with the soil attached. This helps ease the transition into the terrarium.

3 A SERRATED KNIFE: You may need it to release the moss if there are rocks or other plants growing nearby. Make sure not to damage tree roots in the process.

4 PLASTIC ZIP-TOP BAGS: You'll need a place to put the moss, and you may want to separate it by type.

5 A SHIM OR RULER: A shim or ruler helps to get some leverage when lifting large pieces of moss, plus a ruler comes in handy if you ever need to make sure the moss will fit well in a particular terrarium.

6 MOSQUITO/TICK PROTECTION: 'Nough said.

7 WATER: You might get thirsty, and it's handy for a rinse in case you touch something gross.

8 GOOD SHOES: We learned this lesson the hard way. Michelle once surrendered her shoe to a persnickety bog while mossin'. Be sure your feet are protected by boots or reeeally good grippy shoes, or you may find yourself walking back barefoot.

9 A FRIEND: Is it necessary? It's a good idea. Should anything happen, from an injury to an asthma attack, somebody's got your back.

10 KNOWLEDGE: Does the area have bears or bobcats? Be careful of where you go and what you disturb or you may *really* wind up as yeti food!

Keep in mind that some moss peels up off the ground easily, but other moss is more firmly entrenched. If so, use your trowel or knife to cut vertically into the ground around the section of moss you want, then use the trowel or shim to remove the desired moss. Moss is typically rooted in the soil about a half inch to three inches (12 millimeters to 7.5 centimeters) deep. Remove any debris from the moss and gently place it in a plastic bag. Then spray your moss thoroughly with pesticide (see page 32). (If you simply can't find moss anywhere nearby, check the Resources on page 116 for information on where to buy moss.)

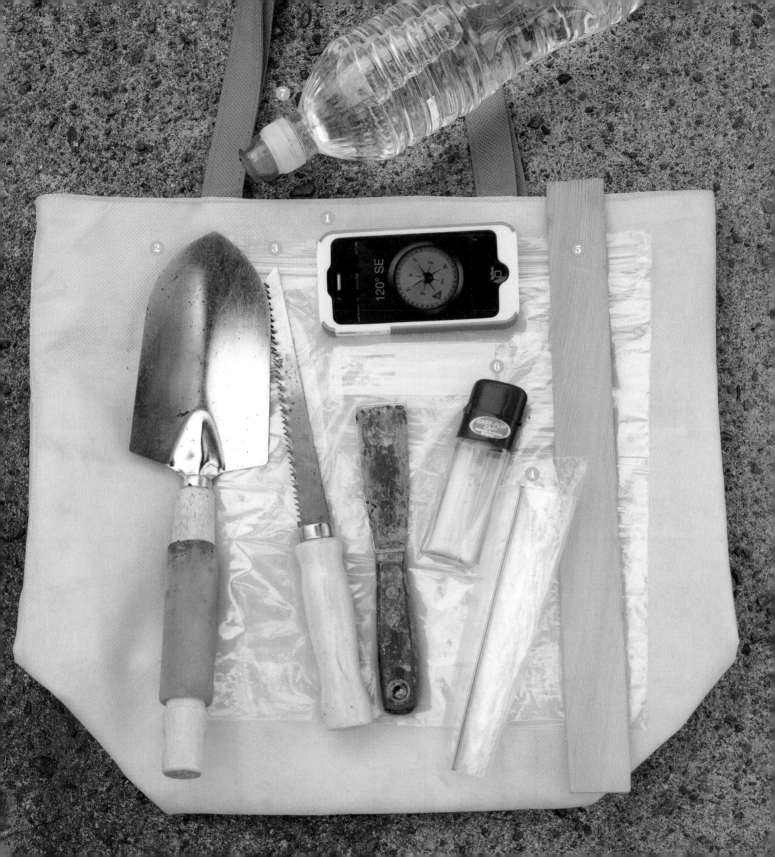

BEYOND MOSS: OTHER PLANTS FOR TERRARIUMS

There is a world of plants beyond moss for landscaping a terrarium.

Drop by your local nursery and talk to the staff about the availability of plants you'd like to include, as some plants are simply not available year-round. This list is by no means exhaustive, but it's a good place to start.

SUN-LOVING PLANTS

boxleaf euonymus (*Euonymus japonicus 'Microphyllus Aureovariegatus'*)

boxwood (*Buxus sempervirens*)

brass buttons (*Leptinella potentillina verdigris*)

carpet violet (*Alsobia [episcea] dianthiflora*)

Chinese pepper tree (*Zanthoxylum odorum*)

croton (*Codiaeum variegatum*)

dwarf arctic birch (*Betula nana*)

dwarf nutgrass (*Eleocharis radicans* dwarf)

dwarf snow bush (*Breynia disticha nana*)

English ivy (*Hedera helix misty*) or gnome Ivy (*Hedera helix spetchley*); also several others (feen finger, mini Easter, oak leaf, silver king)

Joseph's coat (*Alternanthera ficoidea*) in several small varieties and colors

miniature grape ivy (*Cissus Striata*)

peperomia (*Peperomia minima*)

pineapple verbena (*Nashia inaguensis*)

quilted creeping fig (*Ficus Pumila Repens Minima*) or snowflake variety

snow rose (white or pink, single- or double-blooming serissa)

sweet flag varieties (*Acorus gramineus minima aurea, Acorus gramineus* dwarf *himemasamume*)

twiggy spikemoss (*Selaginella sanguinolenta* var. *compressa*)

SHADE-LOVING PLANTS

gnome ivy (*Hedera helix spetchley*); fine in shade, but the leaves will grow up to one inch (2.5 centimeters) in the sun and may crowd out other plants

golden clubmoss

Irish or Scottish moss (*Sagina subulata*)

Krauss' spikemoss, or trailing spikemoss (*Selaginella kraussiana*)

miniature "shamrock" ivy (*Hedera helix shamrock*)

miniature ferns (we like several miniature fern varieties but prefer asparagus [*plumosus*] ferns)

ORCHIDS

bromeliads and epiphytes

jewel orchid (*Ludisia discolor*)

Phalaenopsis violacea (malaysia x var. *borneo)*

Phalaenopsis violacea borneo

SUCCULENTS

Aeonium arboreum (turns reddish with lots of sun)
or *Aeonium haworthii*

baby's toes (*Fenestraria rhopalophylla*)

dwarf cowhorn agave (*Agave cupreata*)

gollum (*Crassula ovata gollum*) and variegated jade
(*Crassula ovata variegata*); any crassula, really!

Haworthia coarcata (likes some shade)

hens and chicks (*Sempervivum*)

jade or money tree (*Crassula ovata*)

lizard's tail (*Crassula muscosa*); caution: this succulent
can grow to a foot (30.5 centimeters) tall

miniature aloe (*Aloe haworthioides*)

miniature pine tree (*Crassula tetragona*)

panda plant (*Kalanchoe tomentosa*)

pinwheel aeonium (*Aeonium haworthii*)

rosary vine (*Crassula rupestris*)

sedum (one cutey is *Sedum burrito*, aka burrow's tail
sedum, and another is *Sedum rubrotinctum*, aka
the jellybean plant

tree aeonium (*Aeonium arboreum*); turns reddish
with lots of sun

zipper plant (*Euphorbia anoplia*)

CARNIVOROUS PLANTS

Mexican butterwort plant (*Pinguicula moranensis*)

yellow trumpet pitcher (*Sarracenia flava*)

fork-leaved sundew (*Drosera binata*)

Venus flytrap (*Dionaea muscipula*)

1. **CRASSULA OVATA**

2. **SEDUM PACHYPHYLLUM**

3. **HAWTHORIA COARCATA**

4. **SEDUM ALBUM**

5. **SEDUM BURRITO**

LAYER 5: MINI-SCAPING

To "mini-scape" means to artfully create depth and dimension in your terrarium using rocks, figurines, or anything else that adds a personal touch and creates a miniature world.

ONCE YOUR PLANTS ARE IN PLACE, YOU'RE READY TO START MINI-SCAPING. For best results, we suggest using objects less than three inches (7.5 centimeters) tall, such as dollhouse miniatures, plastic toy figurines, train set or architectural miniatures, or fun stuff from craft stores and discount shops. For more ideas, see the Resources on page 116.

When determining how you're going to mini-scape, first consider the type of greenery you're using. For instance, moss is the perfect choice for creating grassy scenes, while plants create the feel of a thriving jungle, and succulents mimic a desert oasis. You can add jagged rocks that look like mountains or flat rocks to pave a road, as shown above left, or sprinkle decorative sand to make a beach. To create a little river in your new world, as shown above right, try stacking pieces of beach glass and pushing them gently into the dirt. And when you add miniature figurines, the world really starts to come together.

No matter how you mini-scape your world, make sure to use a pokey stick to tuft the moss or soil around an object so it looks as if it's part of the landscape.

ITEMS FOR MINI-SCAPING

WHETHER YOU'RE USING FIGURINES OR ITEMS FOUND IN NATURE TO MINI-SCAPE YOUR TERRARIUM, they all have to be waterproof so they don't grow mold or leach into the soil. We love to use rocks and petrified wood to mini-scape our terrariums. Agate, quartz, crystal, and all of the natural items shown at left are safe to use in your terrarium as is. Just give them a rinse and place them where you'd like. However, some rocks, such as limestone, contain minerals that may leach into the soil, which can harm the mossy goodness there. To be safe, we avoid using any rocks that we don't recognize, or are unfamiliar with. Also note that driftwood will grow mold, and the salt in driftwood (depending on where it comes from and the way you've washed it) may leach into the soil, so it's best to avoid using it in terrariums altogether.

If you'll be including anything porous or that may disintegrate in your terrarium—such as clay figures, wooden coffee stirrers, or our beloved twigs—they will need to be waterproofed. If you are in doubt about any of the items that will go in your terrarium, go ahead and seal them. To waterproof items, use any clear spray-on general-purpose arts-and-crafts sealant, readily available at craft stores. Always follow the directions on the sealant container; they will specify drying times (but typically give each item a day or two to cure). There are some unique products on the market, including rubber and plastic dips, but these aren't necessary.

1. SAND

2. PETRIFIED WOOD

3. PYRITE (TOP) AND BROWN AGATE (BOTTOM)

4. SNAKESKIN JASPER

5. KYANITE

6. FLUORITE

7. SODALITE

8. AMETHYST

9. BEACH GLASS

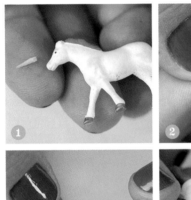

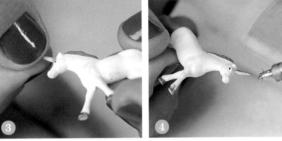

AS YOU REALLY GET INTO TERRARIN' AND START OBSESSING OVER MINIATURES LIKE US TWIG CHICKS, you may find yourself inspired to manipulate your miniatures. After all, why let your materials dictate your creative boundaries? For instance, you can easily turn a regular ol' horse figurine into a unicorn by snipping off the tip of a toothpick, gluing it onto your horse's head, then painting it gold (see above). Or transform a necklace pendant into a shrine (see page 70). We also like to change up the color of our miniatures, or even add a little graffiti (see page 58). We recommend using acrylic or enamel paints, then waterproofing the figurine if the material you painted onto is prone to molding (see page 45).

For hardcore miniature manipulation, you may even want to invest in a "helping hands" tool—a free-standing magnifying glass with a cool grabbing clamp attachment—which is perfect for painting miniatures (see above).

Once you have decorated and sealed the objects you want to include in your terrarium, you'll want them to stay put—especially if your terrarium will be traveling to reach its recipient. To anchor your objects, use extra-strong glue to attach small, galvanized nails to the bottom of each object, then stick them into the soil or moss. This will keep your decorative rocks and cute miniatures from falling off their perches.

CARING FOR YOUR TERRARIUM

Caring for your terrarium is mostly a matter of keeping it in a place with the right amount of light and making sure it's hydrated.

ALL MOSS TERRARIUMS: All mosses need filtered or dappled light, but never direct sunlight. Even artificial light will work fine—a blessing for the cubicle-bound or for folks in basement apartments! Care instructions vary depending on whether your container is open or closed.

On average, closed container moss terrariums require a light misting from a spray bottle every two to four weeks, depending on the amount of light they receive. Condensation is not uncommon, but consistent condensation may be a warning sign: either the terrarium is getting too much moisture, or the terrarium is getting too much sun and the moisture is being drawn out of the moss. If the moss is dry to the touch and there's still a lot of condensation, give your moss a healthy misting, leave the lid off for about an hour to let the additional moisture evaporate, and move the terrarium to a shadier spot.

While we do not recommend fully open containers for moss, we have been known to use laboratory glass such as Erlenmeyer and Florence flasks; both have narrow openings that hold in moisture well enough. These simply need to be monitored more closely to check for dehydration and misted every one to three weeks.

PLANT TERRARIUMS: You need to make sure the plants inside are given the specific conditions they need. For instance, shade-loving plants will need to be watered less often than sun-worshipping plants. Most ferns enjoy a moist atmosphere, while many plants need to dry out before rewatering; a plant that constantly sits in water will be at risk for fungus diseases and root rot. Note that many plants require fertilizer at some point.

Find out what your plant needs, and make sure it gets it. Study labels as you shop for plants and always remember that designing a terrarium dedicated to plants with similar needs will make for a happy ecosystem.

SUCCULENT TERRARIUMS: Succulents vary widely in their needs depending on their type, so it's best to consult your local nursery or read a succulent-care guide to learn how to tend to yours. Most "succers" like to be entirely dry before a watering. Succulents are very hardy little fellows, but this also means they show signs of unhappiness over a period of months rather than days. If a succulent is underwatered or overwatered, it will start to look like a weird husk of its happy self. We tend to water our succulents every two weeks, but it's really whenever the soil is dry. Under no circumstance should a succulent sit in water.

Terrariums

GALORE

The terrariums in this section are meant to get your creative juices flowing. We included a materials list with each one so you can copy what you see, or you can use this gallery as an inspirational jumping-off point to create your own unique tiny green world.

SOAKING UP RAYS (PREVIOUS PAGE)

This glass vase has the perfect sandy spot for our little sun chaser!

CONTAINER: New vase

FOUNDATION ROCKS: Base layer of pebbles

FILTRATION: Typical filtration moss (dried sheet moss)

SOIL: Peat moss mixture

MINI-SCAPING: Sheet moss, mood moss, and reindeer moss; sand for beach; sunbather figurine

THE LAST UNICORN

This legendary creature rears up to survey his mossy kingdom along the glittering waters of his little green world.

CONTAINER: New apothecary jar

FOUNDATION ROCKS: Base layer of pebbles

FILTRATION: Typical filtration moss (dried sheet moss)

SOIL: Peat moss mixture

MINI-SCAPING: Mood moss, reindeer moss, sheet moss, and sphagnum moss; petrified wood as rock formation; blue gems for water; unicorn figurine

CAPTURED FAIRY

In this magical world of sphagnum moss trees and towering twigs, a flitting fairy alights upon a sliver of agate.

CONTAINER: New apothecary jar

FOUNDATION ROCKS: Base layer of pebbles

FILTRATION: Typical filtration moss (dried sheet moss)

SOIL: Peat moss mixture

MINI-SCAPING: Pillow moss, sphagnum moss, and reindeer moss; polished agate slice with rough edges; twigs; fairy figurine

OUT OF TOWNERS

On a very green corner of the mossy isle of Manhattan, we meet a couple that found some trouble on vacation.

CONTAINER: New apothecary jar

FOUNDATION ROCKS: Base layer of pebbles

FILTRATION: Typical filtration moss (dried sheet moss)

SOIL: Peat moss mixture

MINI-SCAPING: Mood moss, pillow moss, sheet moss, and reindeer moss; plaster sidewalk and brick wall with hand-painted graffiti; two tourists, police officer, bag lady, and lampost figurines

TENDING THE FLOCK

Here, a stoic man and his dog watch over a herd of sheep wandering along the verdant countryside.

CONTAINER: New apothecary jar

FOUNDATION ROCKS: Base layer of pebbles

FILTRATION: Typical filtration moss (dried sheet moss)

SOIL: Peat moss mixture

MINI-SCAPING: Pillow moss, mood moss, sheet moss, reindeer moss, sphagnum moss, and asparagus fern; petrified wood as rock formation; twig; sheep, sheep dog, and herder figurines

THE ENGLISH COUNTRYSIDE

Take a peek inside the rolling hills of an English estate. The lord and lady feed the ducks and swans at the pond while the captain and his hunting dogs pass into the woods beyond a whitewashed wall.

CONTAINER: New apothecary jar

FOUNDATION ROCKS: Base layer of pebbles

FILTRATION: Typical filtration moss (dried sheet moss)

SOIL: Peat moss mixture

MINI-SCAPING: Pillow moss, mood moss, sheet moss, reindeer moss, and sphagnum moss; blue glass for pond; miniature white wall and bench; woman with parasol, man, captain atop a horse, dogs, ducks, and swan figurines

DINO-SAUR US!

Our little guy barely escapes the clutches of ravenous raptors that somehow exist in the modern world!

CONTAINER: New apothecary jar

FOUNDATION ROCKS: Base layer of pebbles

FILTRATION: Typical filtration moss (dried sheet moss)

SOIL: Peat moss mixture

MINI-SCAPING: Pillow moss and mood moss; small pebbles for landscaping; disabled electric fence (tee-hee); dinosaur and man figurines

ADVENTURERS

In this desert world, a group of hikers have wandered a bit too far off the beaten path . . . and into a terrarium! Some set up camp while their pals climb the face of a cliff. Alienlike succulents add life to a barren land.

CONTAINER: Large vintage bowl

FOUNDATION ROCKS: Base layer of pebbles

FILTRATION: Typical filtration moss (dried sheet moss)

SOIL: Succulent mixture

MINI-SCAPING: Various succulents in bloom; petrified wood as mountain and rock formations; small pebbles for landscaping; sand for desert; hiker figurines

ACOUSTIC (OPPOSITE)

In a small, succulent world lives a tiny busker, playing his guitar in the wasteland for two bits and a smile.

CONTAINER: Recycled glass container

FOUNDATION ROCKS: Pea gravel

FILTRATION: Typical filtration moss (dried sheet moss)

SOIL: Succulent mixture

MINI-SCAPING: Sedum succulent; pea gravel; sand for desert; man-with-guitar figurine

PLAYTIME! (ABOVE)

This open, succulent terrarium features fun-loving kids on a seesaw and in a sandbox!

CONTAINER: New glass vase

FOUNDATION ROCKS: Base layer of pebbles

FILTRATION: Typical filtration moss (dried sheet moss)

SOIL: Succulent mixture

MINI-SCAPING: Burro's tail; petrified wood as rock foundation; sand for playground; miniature seesaw and sandbox; children and mom figurines

NIWA (PREVIOUS SPREAD)

A Shinto shrine overlooks a Zen garden, where a lovely geisha surveys the grounds of her moss valley.

CONTAINER: New apothecary jar

FOUNDATION ROCKS: Base layer of pebbles

FILTRATION: Typical filtration moss (dried sheet moss)

SOIL: Peat moss mixture

MINI-SCAPING: Pillow moss, mood moss, reindeer moss, sphagnum moss, and sheet moss; a Shinto shrine (this was once a necklace pendant); petrified wood as rock formation; blue glass for pond; geisha and swan figurines

PICTURE THAT!

Dearest photographer . . . we put you on a pedestal so that you may have a better vantage point. Snap away!

CONTAINER: New cupcake stand

FOUNDATION ROCKS: Base layer of small pebbles

FILTRATION: Typical filtration moss (dried sheet moss)

SOIL: Peat moss mixture

MINI-SCAPING: Pillow moss, sphagnum moss, and reindeer moss; petrified wood as rock formation; a cute lil' twig; photographer figurine

TENDING THE LAWN (OPPOSITE)

Meet the proud owners of a tiny world inside of a cupcake dish. These folks tend to their garden with love and devotion, raking the grassy expanse of pillow moss and pruning reindeer moss bushes.

CONTAINER: New cupcake glass container

FOUNDATION ROCKS: Pea gravel

FILTRATION: Typical filtration moss (dried sheet moss)

SOIL: Peat moss mixture

MINI-SCAPING: Mood moss, reindeer moss, and pillow moss; man and woman (with rake) figurines

OLGA & FRITZ (ABOVE)

A frolicking fräulein and her beau traipse along the Alps, dancing to a tune all their own. Ah, the hills are alive with the sound of music!

CONTAINER: New apothecary jar

FOUNDATION ROCKS: Base layer of pebbles

FILTRATION: Typical filtration moss (dried sheet moss)

SOIL: Peat moss mixture

MINI-SCAPING: Pillow moss, mood moss, reindeer moss, and sphagnum moss; petrified wood as mountain; German dancing figurines

TEENSY WORLD (ABOVE)

In this unbelievably small glass world, two young explorers look out in wonder.

CONTAINER: Vintage Chanel perfume bottle

FOUNDATION ROCKS: Pea gravel

FILTRATION: Typical filtration moss (dried sheet moss)

SOIL: Peat moss mixture

MINI-SCAPING: Mood moss and sphagnum moss; two child figurines

PISS OFF (OPPOSITE)

Our favorite mohawked dude! He's pissed, but we're sure he has his reasons. A lightbulb-shaped bud vase is the perfect home for our angry punk rocker.

CONTAINER: Lightbulb-shaped bud vase

FOUNDATION ROCKS: Pea gravel

FILTRATION: Typical filtration moss (dried sheet moss)

SOIL: Peat moss mixture

MINI-SCAPING: Sheet moss, mood moss, and reindeer moss; punk-rock figurine

THE PERFECT VIEW (OPPOSITE)

Within a vintage cookie jar is the perfect view into a lush world. The sodalite lake is full of jumpin' fish and our patient fisherman waits to catch one.

CONTAINER: Vintage cookie jar

FOUNDATION ROCKS: Base layer of pebbles

FILTRATION: Typical filtration moss (dried sheet moss)

SOIL: Peat moss mixture

MINI-SCAPING: Pillow moss, mood moss, reindeer moss, and sphagnum moss; petrified wood as rock formation; sodalite slab as lake; twig; man in boat and bird figurines

VERDANT PERSPECTIVE (ABOVE)

This large handblown glass is designed to "drip" off the shelf. It contains an inspired artist at his easel, painting the world before him.

CONTAINER: Handblown glass with small opening

FOUNDATION ROCKS: Base layer of pebbles

FILTRATION: Typical filtration moss (dried sheet moss)

SOIL: Peat moss mixture

MINI-SCAPING: Mood moss, sheet moss, and reindeer moss; artist-at-easel figurine

DUCK, DUCK, GOOSE (PREVIOUS PAGE)

A little girl tends to her feathered friends at a pond in this open terrarium filled with papyrus and mosses.

CONTAINER: Vintage glass vase

FOUNDATION ROCKS: Base layer of pebbles

FILTRATION: Typical filtration moss (dried sheet moss)

SOIL: Peat moss mixture

MINI-SCAPING: Papyrus plant, reindeer moss, and mood moss; petrified wood as rock formation; small pebbles for landscaping; geese and girl figurines

THE HAPPIEST DAY

It's a brand-new life for this happy couple, emerging from their wedding arbor to greet the world!

CONTAINER: New apothecary jar

FOUNDATION ROCKS: Base layer of pebbles

FILTRATION: Typical filtration moss (dried sheet moss)

SOIL: Peat moss mixture

MINI-SCAPING: Mood moss, sheet moss, pillow moss, reindeer moss, and sphagnum moss; petrified wood as rock formation; twigs; small handmade arbor from plastic parts; bride and groom figurines

PRINCE CHARMING

The love of a gallant prince and glamorous princess flourish while taking a stroll on the grounds of a glorious castle.

CONTAINER: New apothecary jar

FOUNDATION ROCKS: Base layer of pebbles

FILTRATION: Typical filtration moss (dried sheet moss)

SOIL: Peat moss mixture

MINI-SCAPING: Reindeer moss, mood moss, pillow moss, and sheet moss; petrified wood as rock formation; a small fancy fence and a miniature castle (normally used for aquariums); prince and princess figurines

THE WILD WILD WEST

In the shadow of a petrified-wood mountain, this wind-whipped cowboy is outrun by the thumping hooves of a herd of buffalo on the plains of the wild West.

CONTAINER: New glass container

FOUNDATION ROCKS: Base layer of pebbles

FILTRATION: Typical filtration moss (dried sheet moss)

SOIL: Peat moss mixture

MINI-SCAPING: Pillow moss, mood moss, reindeer moss, and sheet moss; large petrified wood as mountain; cowboy and buffalo figurines

OUR PRIVATE GALA (FOLLOWING PAGE)

Perched delicately on a cake stand, an elegant dancing couple glides to their own symphony along a smooth slice of agate.

CONTAINER: Glass cake stand

FOUNDATION ROCKS: Base layer of pebbles

FILTRATION: Typical filtration moss (dried sheet moss)

SOIL: Peat moss mixture

MINI-SCAPING: Pillow moss, mood moss, haircap moss, reindeer moss, and sphagnum moss; a fun twig; petrified wood as rock formation; agate slab as dance floor; two dancing figurines

THE LAND BEFORE TIME (ABOVE)

In the time of cavemen, two wandering dinosaurs devour the foliage of a lush forest. We purchased these dinosaur figures at a discount store, but then painted them to look more realistic.

CONTAINER: Vintage vase

FOUNDATION ROCKS: Base layer of pebbles

FILTRATION: Typical filtration moss (dried sheet moss)

SOIL: Peat moss mixture

MINI-SCAPING: Young boxwood, ivy, reindeer moss, and usnea lichen branch; petrified wood as rock formation; dinosaur figurines

FIGHT FOR YOUR RIGHT! (OPPOSITE)

Marching for peace, these little activists are heard loud and clear as they march to town!

CONTAINER: Vintage globe

FOUNDATION ROCKS: Base layer of pebbles

FILTRATION: Typical filtration moss (dried sheet moss)

SOIL: Peat moss mixture

MINI-SCAPING: Asparagus fern and variegated ivy; protester figurines with hand-painted banner

SERENGETI

Within this large dome-shaped terrarium, you'll catch a contained glimpse into the wild, including giraffes at a watering hole, a herd of zebras, a skulking lion, and a towering tree with tiny monkeys!

CONTAINER: Large helmet-shaped glass pedestal with cloche

FOUNDATION ROCKS: Base layer of rocks

FILTRATION: Typical filtration moss (dried sheet moss)

SOIL: Peat moss mixture

MINI-SCAPING: Pillow moss, reindeer moss, and mood moss; petrified wood as mountain formations; blue beach and sea glass as watering hole; an array of miniature wild animals; and a happy twig!

TINY WORLDS (ABOVE)

On a northern-facing windowsill live all these tiny worlds in the shape of songbirds, a ribbiting frog, and a turvy-topsy cube. Each tiny thing contains an intricately mini-scaped world.

CONTAINER: Various bud vases

FOUNDATION ROCKS: Base layer of pea gravel

FILTRATION: Typical filtration moss (dried sheet moss)

SOIL: Peat moss mixture

MINI-SCAPING: Mood moss, sheet moss, and reindeer moss; swimmer and businessman figurines

OVER THE RIVER (OPPOSITE)

Cross the bridge over the river and walk into the woods, where a towering orchid stems from the fertile ground.

CONTAINER: New glass vase

FOUNDATION ROCKS: Base layer of pebbles

FILTRATION: Typical filtration moss (dried sheet moss)

SOIL: Orchid bark

MINI-SCAPING: Reindeer moss and a beach of usnea lichen; Phalaenopsis orchid; beach glass as stream; petrified wood as rock formation; ceramic bridge

THE GREAT ESCAPE

Within a repurposed gumball machine, our little prisoner is plotting his escape!

CONTAINER: Vintage gumball machine (the inside must be waterproofed)

FOUNDATION ROCKS: Base layer of pebbles

FILTRATION: Typical filtration moss (dried sheet moss)

SOIL: Peat moss mixture

MINI-SCAPING: Mood moss, pillow moss, sheet moss, reindeer moss, and sphagnum buds; prisoner figurine

DON'T FEAR THE REAPER

Death looms in a tiny graveyard housed within our favorite little glass egg.

CONTAINER: Vintage glass egg

FOUNDATION ROCKS: Base layer of pebbles

FILTRATION: Typical filtration moss (dried sheet moss)

SOIL: Peat moss mixture

MINI-SCAPING: Sheet moss, pillow moss, and reindeer moss; petrified wood as rock formation; crosses (made from coffee stirrers); grim reaper figurine

TALES OF THE TRAILER PARK

This couple lives amid a lush forest of plants and reindeer moss in their tiny trailer. Hubbie's found a cool spot in the front yard to drink a brew while his wife looks on in disapproval and yells about the garbage!

CONTAINER: New glass vase

FOUNDATION ROCKS: Base layer of pebbles

FILTRATION: Typical filtration moss (dried sheet moss)

SOIL: Potting soil

MINI-SCAPING: Meadow rue, lichen, and reindeer moss; petrified wood as rock formation; man and woman figurines; miniature trailer and assorted "trash"

OASIS

A trio of camels works its way through the Egyptian desert and finds a small oasis of succulents in the sand.

CONTAINER: Vintage compote base

FOUNDATION ROCKS: Base layer of pebbles

FILTRATION: Typical filtration moss (dried sheet moss)

SOIL: Succulent mixture

MINI-SCAPING: Succulents (burro's tail, *Haworthia attenuata*, and jade plant); sand for desert; petrified wood as rock formation; camel figurines

THRILL OF THE HUNT

A pack of ravenous wolves encircles a struggling buck while howls echo in the air.

CONTAINER: New apothecary jar

FOUNDATION ROCKS: Base layer of pebbles

FILTRATION: Typical filtration moss (dried sheet moss)

SOIL: Peat moss mixture

MINI-SCAPING: Pillow moss, mood moss, reindeer moss, and sheet moss; petrified wood as rock formation; wolves and deer figurines

HANG TEN! (ABOVE)

This surfin' Sally makes waves! As she crests a wave, she sees the sandy beach and verdant valley that lies beyond. Gnarly!

CONTAINER: New apothecary jar

FOUNDATION ROCKS: Base layer of pebbles

FILTRATION: Typical filtration moss (dried sheet moss)

SOIL: Peat moss mixture

MINI-SCAPING: Pillow moss, sheet moss, mood moss, reindeer moss, and sphagnum moss; petrified wood as rock formation; blue beach glass as ocean; sand for beach; surfer girl figurine

SEASICK SONATA (OPPOSITE)

Party on the beach in this handblown glass terrarium! These little guys enjoy the sand in their toes while they play in time with the crashing waves.

CONTAINER: Handblown glass

FOUNDATION ROCKS: Base layer of pebbles

FILTRATION: Typical filtration moss (dried sheet moss)

SOIL: Peat moss mixture

MINI-SCAPING: Mood moss, sheet moss, and reindeer moss; sand for beach; band member figurines

ART IN THE BIG APPLE

Housed within a vintage glass apple we find a sculptor chiseling perfection from marble.
His masterpiece is slowly revealed as he works along the banks of a beach glass river.

CONTAINER: Vintage apple-shaped glass with removable lid

FOUNDATION ROCKS: Base layer of pebbles

FILTRATION: Typical filtration moss (dried sheet moss)

SOIL: Peat moss mixture

MINI-SCAPING: Mood moss, sheet moss, pillow moss, and reindeer moss; petrified wood
as rock formation; blue beach glass as river; sculptor figurine; miniature sculpture

CATCH OF THE DAY (ABOVE)

Within a handblown world, a fisherman on a cliff casts a line into sea glass waters while a silly goose looks on.

CONTAINER: Handblown glass

FOUNDATION ROCKS: Base layer of pebbles

FILTRATION: Typical filtration moss (dried sheet moss)

SOIL: Peat moss mixture

MINI-SCAPING: Mood moss and reindeer moss; petrified wood as a cliff; beach glass and sea glass as water; fisherman and goose figurines

SUSPENDED WORLDS (OPPOSITE)

Small glass globes hang suspended in air. One world contains succulents and a lady lounging on a park bench. The other contains a grouping of ivy and reindeer moss.

CONTAINER: New hanging glass spheres

FOUNDATION ROCKS: Pea gravel as base layer

FILTRATION: Typical filtration moss (dried sheet moss)

SOIL: Succulent mix for succulents; peat moss mix for plants

MINI-SCAPING: Succulent terrarium: sedum succulents, girl figurine, and miniature bench; Ivy terrarium: ivy and reindeer moss

MAD SCIENTIST

We love to repurpose glass items for terrarin'; here is a selection of laboratory glass, including a vintage tripod for a boiling flask, and a variety of Erlenmeyer flasks.

CONTAINER: Vintage laboratory glass

FOUNDATION ROCKS: Base layer of pebbles

FILTRATION: Typical filtration moss (dried sheet moss)

SOIL: Peat moss mixture

MINI-SCAPING: Mood moss, sheet moss, and reindeer moss; sheep, monkey, and mime figurines; twigs

TOXIC SPILL

A hazmat team works diligently in a succulent desert to clean up a toxic spill.

CONTAINER: Large handblown glass

FOUNDATION ROCKS: Base layer of pebbles

FILTRATION: Typical filtration moss (dried sheet moss)

SOIL: Succulent mixture

MINI-SCAPING: Jade plant, burro's tail and usnea lichen branch; petrified wood as rock formations; beach glass as water; coarse gravel; sand; hazmat worker figurines

HERE ARE SPECIFIC SUGGESTIONS FOR FINDING THE MATERIALS TO MAKE YOUR OWN TERRARIUM!
If you don't want to commit to buying all of these materials in bulk, Twig Terrariums sells DIY Kits with all the ingredients in smaller portions so that you can create just one little green world . . . or two . . . okay, or maybe even three. Each kit comes complete with glass, moss, a cute little terrarium dweller, as well as soil, filtration, and rocks. Oh yes, it also includes assembly and care instructions! To order online, check out www.twigterrariums.com.

CONTAINERS:
We love to use antique glass for our terrariums. Antique malls in remote locales will usually give you more bang for your buck. For non-antique containers, we like to head to local bargain shops and 99-cent stores, which can provide interesting glass containers. For modern shapes, check out big-box shops, including IKEA, Crate & Barrel, and The Container Store. If you're curious about having a piece of glass custom-blown for your terrarium, check online for nearby glassblowers to avoid having to ship the container. And of course, don't overlook your own home! Old canning jars, bottlenecked glass vases, compotes, and even spice jars work nicely.

ROCKS, FILTRATION, SOIL, AND TOOLS:
Almost all of the tools and materials used for the terrariums in this book can be found at garden supply centers and hardware superstores. If you cannot find what you are looking for locally, try these online sources:
www.homedepot.com
www.lowes.com

For long tweezers, mechanical fingers, and the helping hands magnifying glass, check out www.amazon.com.

MOSS, SUCCULENTS, AND PLANTS:
It's always best to buy plants in person at a local garden supply shop or hardware superstore so that you can check their health and transport them home gently. Although moss is available online, most of it comes in huge quantities, so we suggest that you collect your own moss from nature (see page 38). If collecting your own moss is not a possibility, then check www.ebay.com for folks that sell lovely moss (though it might cost a pretty penny).

FIGURINES FOR MINI-SCAPING:
We use all kinds of figurines for mini-scaping, such as dollhouse miniatures, plastic toys from toy stores and 99-cent stores, and train set and architectural miniatures. If you can't find what you're looking for locally at stores like Michaels or Hobby Lobby, try these online sources:

For dollhouse miniatures, try www.minimumworld .com. Be sure to check sizes, since dollhouse miniatures can be larger than you might think!

For ceramic bonsai figurines, try www.bonsaiboy.com.

When in doubt, check out www.ebay.com and even www.etsy.com for little terrarium dwellers!

Happy terraring, folks!

MICHELLE INCIARRANO is a full-time fine art student, avid reader, and passionate Brooklynite. She is married and raises two very spoiled animals: a cocker spaniel named Maxwell's Silver Hammer (after the Beatles song) and a big brown bunny rabbit named Harley. Michelle has been supporting herself and independently exploring her creative side since she was sixteen years old. She's had an interest in botany since early childhood, so terrariums came naturally to her, but landscaping miniature worlds is driven by her artistic flair. Her other passions include photography (for which she's been credited in several publications), scrapbooking, card making, and steampunk art, but most of her time is now happily spent creating small green worlds with Katy.

KATY MASLOW, a born and bred Brooklynite, took to fleeing the borough in her early years. Humoring her wanderlust, she has lived all across the country, including long stints in "Colorful Colorado" and "Virginia Is for Lovers." She studied poetry with the ghost of Allen Ginsberg at Brooklyn College and received her BFA in creative writing. Her poetry and photography have appeared in a smattering of journals, though nowadays her time is mostly spent land- scaping miniature worlds with her pal Michelle. She currently resides in a forgotten corner of Brooklyn with her two cats, Herman and Roscoe, and is an avid reader, writer, and bone collector. When not hard at work or play, you can find her feeding the birds, shopping for terrarable glass, or ogling oddities.

The Twig Chicks have a lot to be thankful for! We would like to acknowledge all our family and friends (you know who you are!) for offering support and encouragement as we traipse along our Twiggy path. Thanks also to our loyal fans, who we've turned into moss addicts. We give much love and respect to plant nerds and mossophiles the world over! We owe special thanks to our rockstar editor at ABRAMS, Wesley Royce; our amazing photographer, Robert Wright (www.robertwrightphoto.com); our stunning photo stylist, Karen Schaupeter; our literary agent, Jim McCarthy of Dystel & Goderich; Michelle's chemistry professor at Brooklyn College, Jeremiah Murphy; Sean Gilvey for the handblown glass that appears on pages 106 and 110; and Katy's cat Herman, for staying still while Robert took his picture!

Published in 2012 by Stewart, Tabori & Chang
An imprint of ABRAMS

Copyright © 2012 Michelle Inciarrano and Katy Maslow
Photographs copyright © 2012 Robert Wright

Library of Congress Cataloging-in-Publication Data

Inciarrano, Michelle.
 Tiny world terrariums : a step-by-step guide to easily
contained life /
Michelle Inciarrano and Katy Maslow.
    p. cm.
 Step-by-step guide to easily contained life
 ISBN 978-1-58479-964-1
1. Terrariums. 2. Miniature craft. I. Maslow, Katy. II.
Title. III.
Title: Step-by-step guide to easily contained life.
 SB417.I53 2012
 635.9'824—dc23
                     2011045353

Editor: Wesley Royce with Liana Allday
Designer: Kwasi Osei and Danielle Young
Art Director: Michelle Ishay-Cohen
Production Manager: Ankur Ghosh

The text of this book was composed in Rockwell, Gotham,
and Eames Century Modern.

Printed and bound in the U.S.A.

10 9 8 7 6 5 4 3 2 1

Stewart, Tabori & Chang books are available at special
discounts when purchased in quantity for premiums and
promotions as well as fundraising or educational use. Special
editions can also be created to specification. For details,
contact specialsales@abramsbooks.com or the address below.

115 West 18th Street
New York, NY 10011
www.abramsbooks.com